'93

Kwanzaa

Dorothy Rhodes Freeman
and
Dianne M. MacMillan

Reading Consultant:

Michael P. French, Ph.D.,
Bowling Green State University

—Best Holiday Books—

ENSLOW PUBLISHERS, INC.

Bloy St. & Ramsey Ave.	P.O. Box 38
Box 777	Aldershot
Hillside, N.J. 07205	Hants GU12 6BP
U.S.A.	U.K.

Acknowledgement

The authors wish to thank the people at the African American Cultural Center of Los Angeles, California, for reviewing the manuscript, and for providing information and photographs of their Kwanzaa celebration.

Also, our thanks to John Kiango, Swahili Language Instructor at Columbia University, for his review of the Swahili language and pronunciations used in the text.

Library of Congress Cataloging-in-Publication Data

Freeman, Dorothy Rhodes.
    Kwanzaa / Dorothy Rhodes Freeman and Dianne M. MacMillan.
        p. cm. — (Best holiday books)
    Includes index.
    Summary: Introduces the African American holiday begun in 1966
which celebrates seven important principles.
    ISBN 0-89490-381-0
        1. Kwanzaa—Juvenile literature. 2. Afro-Americans—Social life
and customs—Juvenile literature. [1. Kwanzaa. 2. Afro-Americans—
Social life and customs.] I. MacMillan, Dianne M. II. Title.
III. Series.
GT4403.F74 1992
    394.2'68—dc20   91-43100
                                                CIP
                                              AC

48p

Printed in the United States of America

10 9 8 7 6 5 4 3 2 1

Illustration Credits: African American Cultural Center, p. 8; African American Cultural Center/Mpinduzi Khuthaza, pp. 4, 28, 41; Bonnie Rhodes, pp. 6, 10, 13, 17, 20, 22, 25, 27, 29, 32, 33, 35, 36, 37, 39; Patricia Woodhull, p. 16

Cover Illustration: Charlott Nathan

Contents

These people are lighting the Kwanzaa candles. The celebration is at the African American Cultural Center in Los Angeles.

The Holiday Kwanzaa

Kwanzaa (KWAHN-zah) is an African American holiday. It lasts seven days. The first day is December 26. The last day is January 1. It celebrates the African past of black people. It is also about their life in America.

Kwanzaa is a time for families. Families spend time together every day during Kwanzaa. People wear bright African-style clothes. They eat African food and listen to African music. They talk about their grandparents and great-grandparents.

The word "kwanza" is Swahili. Swahili is an African language that many Africans understand. In Swahili, kwanza means first. It stands for the first fruits picked at harvest time.

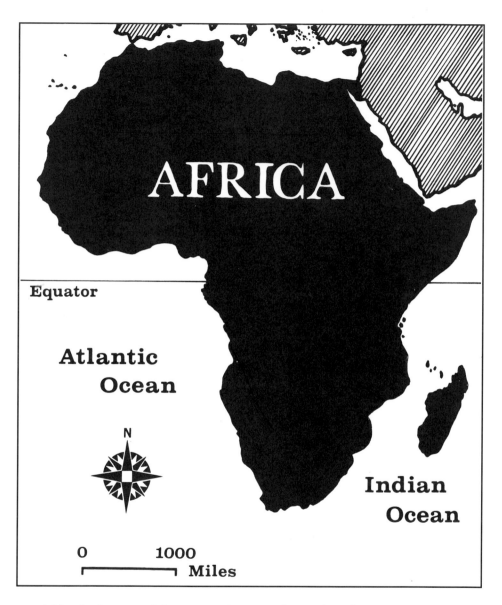

AFRICA

Equator

Atlantic
Ocean

Indian
Ocean

N

0   1000
Miles

Africa is the second largest continent on the earth. It has many kinds of
land, from desert to jungle. People in Africa live many different ways.

This holiday began in 1966. At that time, a holiday program was planned by Dr. Maulana Karenga. Seven children wanted to hold signs spelling Kwanza. But there were only six letters. An "a" was added to "Kwanza." The holiday's name became Kwanzaa. Each child had a letter to hold.

Dr. Maulana Karenga started the celebration of Kwanzaa with his family and friends. Now the holiday is celebrated by millions of people.

How Kwanzaa Began

Dr. Maulana Karenga is an African American leader. He teaches at California State University at Long Beach. In the 1960s he thought that African Americans did not know about their history. He wanted them to be proud of their past. He also thought that African Americans needed to build stronger families. He wanted families to share ideas and grow closer. Dr. Karenga decided to start a holiday that would meet these goals.

First he studied many groups of African people. In every group there was a "first fruits," or harvest, holiday. The holidays were called different names. But in every holiday people did some of the same things. They came together.

They thanked God for giving them food and a good life. They remembered their parents, grandparents, aunts, and uncles who had died. They judged how they lived the past year. They made plans for the new year. They sang, danced, and ate food together.

Dr. Karenga wanted Kwanzaa to be like harvest holidays in Africa. Some of those holidays lasted three days. Some lasted nine

Some African people live together in villages like a family. They work together to raise and harvest crops.

days. Most of them were seven days long. Dr. Karenga liked having a seven day holiday. One group of people in the southern part of Africa had a holiday at the end of the year. They celebrated for seven days until the new year began. Dr. Karenga thought this would be good for Kwanzaa.

The Seven Days of Kwanzaa

Dr. Karenga found that most African groups were guided by seven rules or principles. He decided to use one of these principles each day of Kwanzaa. By the end of the week, all seven principles would be covered.

The seven principles are called Nguzo Saba (NGOO-zoo SAH-bah).

Nguzo means principles. Saba means seven.

Each day of Kwanzaa families come together. They do some things that Africans did in the African holiday. They also talk about one important principle each day.

Before the holiday begins, the family gets everything ready. They put a straw mat on a table. On top of the mat they put a candle holder with seven candles. Each candle stands for one of the principles. Each day a candle will be lit. The candle in the center is black. Three candles on one side are red. Three candles on the other side are green. The colors of the candles have meanings. The black color is for the African American people. The red is for their struggles,

The candle holder and candles are a part of Kwanzaa. Each of the colors of the candles has an important meaning.

now and in the past. Green is for their hopes for the future. Then the family puts a basket of fruit and vegetables, some ears of corn, and a cup on the table. Next to these there are some gifts for the children. Each of these things stands for an important idea. Now the seven days begin:

◆❖❖❖◆❖❖❖◆

December 26—the first day of Kwanzaa
Umoja (oo-MO-jah)
Umoja means being joined together.

People are united in their feelings. They are together in their ideas. Members of a family feel they belong together.

On the first day of Kwanzaa, a family gets together. Most of the time, this gathering is before the evening meal. But some families have their Kwanzaa ceremony in the morning or the afternoon. A ceremony is a celebration always done the same way.

The family stands by the table with the mat and the candle holder with the seven candles.

When everyone is ready, the black candle is lit. Anyone may light it. The person lighting the candle tells its meaning. He might say, "Today is the first day of Kwanzaa. I light the black candle. It stands for unity. It means being together. Unity is the most important principle. We must join together in our neighborhood. We need unity in our families. Then we will feel close to each other."

After this, everyone in the family takes a turn talking. Each one tells why he or she thinks unity is important.

The next part of the Kwanzaa ceremony remembers family members who have died. Someone picks up a cup. The cup is filled with water or fruit juice. First some of the water or juice is poured into a bowl. This pouring is to honor family members who have died. Then the person drinks from the cup. He or she raises the cup high and says, "Harambee" (ha-RAH-mbee).

Harambee means, "Let's all pull together." That is another way of saying, "Let's all work together."

There are seven candles for Kwanzaa. The black candle in the middle is the first one lit.

Everyone says, "Harambee!" They repeat it seven times. Each time is for one of the seven principles. Then the cup is passed around. Each person drinks from it, but if there is a large group, only the leader drinks from the cup.

Now the names of African American leaders and heros are called out. Everyone thinks about the great things these people did.

The leader raises the cup. He says "Harambee!" and the people answer "Harambee!" They say it seven times.

The ceremony is finished for the night. It is time to eat. After eating, the family sings songs or listens to African music.

◆▞▞◆▞▞◆

December 27—the second day of Kwanzaa
Kujichagulia (koo-jee-cha-goo-LEE-ah)
Kujichagulia means being yourself.

African American people are to think for themselves. They decide what they will say or do. They do not let other people tell them how to live and what to be.

Everyone is ready for the second night. Another person lights the candles. First the black candle is lit again. Then the second candle, a red one, is lit. The person might say, "I'm going to go to school and learn. I want to be a doctor. Some people will say that I can't do it. But I know I can."

All of the family members share their ideas on doing what they think is right for themselves. Once again the family drinks from the cup.

They remember the family members who have died. The children love shouting "Harambee" seven times.

Most African Americans like to wear African-style clothes during Kwanzaa. Men and women wear long, loose shirts. Some wear robes. They may wear caps and head wraps. All of the clothes have bright colors.

Long ago African queens wore their hair in cornrows or small braids. Some people call them plaits. Many African American women and girls like to wear their hair this way.

◆▧◆▧◆

December 28—the third day of Kwanzaa
Ujima (oo-JEE-mah)
Ujima means helping one another.

People cooperate by working together. They help each other solve problems.

On this day the black candle and one of the red candles are lit. These are the candles of the first two days. Now the third candle is lit. It is green. The person who lights the candles might say, "All of us need to help one another. If someone needs food or help, we give it. If someone's home burns down, we all help

During Kwanzaa people wear African-style clothes. Some women wear their hair in cornrows.

rebuild it. We give the family food and clothes. We help with what we have."

The family talks about how they have a duty to help their neighbors. By helping each other, all grow stronger.

After the talk, the family honors relatives who have died. They drink from the cup. Then they eat dinner. Families cook African foods. They might have African chicken stew, fried plantain (similar to a banana), and yams. Often they sit on the floor. They eat the food with their fingers. This is the African way.

◆▨◆▨◆

December 29—The fourth day of Kwanzaa
Ujamaa (oo-jah-MAH)
Ujamaa means sharing.

People share the work. They also share the money they make from working.

The candles of the first three nights are lit. Then the fourth candle is lit. It is a red one. There are now one black, two red and one green candle burning. Parents like to have the children light the candles. A child gets to be the first one to tell about the principle. This helps him or her remember what the principle means. The child lighting the candles this night might say, "Our class needs some new books. Everyone is going to bring some money. Together we will have enough to buy some books. We can all share them."

These children all brought money to school to buy new books. Now they have enough books to share. This is one way Ujamaa works.

The parents might talk about starting a business with some friends. They would share the work and the money. An uncle might share the money from his job with the family. Everyone talks about working and sharing. Then they pour and drink from the cup.

◆▪▪◆▪▪◆

December 30—the fifth day of Kwanzaa
Nia (NEE-ah)
Nia means having a goal or purpose.

People need to have goals. They need a purpose or reason for wanting to reach the goals.

On this fifth night, another green candle is lit. Now five candles are burning.

The mother might speak first tonight. She might say, "I think Nia means having a reason to work or having a goal. My goal is to take care of all of you. The purpose of our family is to love and help one another. The goal of Kwanzaa is to help us learn more about who we are. All of us need to set goals. We need to help each other live better lives."

The children might talk about what they want to be when they grow up. One goal of the father might be to help his children get an education. Everyone else tells about the goals they have or what purpose means for them.

Talking together about goals helps the family feel closer. They understand one another better.

Once more they use the cup and remember grandparents and great-grandparents. They talk about the reasons things were done in the past.

◆❖◆❖◆

December 31—the sixth day of Kwanzaa
Kuumba (koo-UH-mbah)
Kuumba means creating.

People create crafts and music and dances. They are also creative when they make their own neighborhoods more beautiful.

The celebrating of the sixth day of Kwanzaa is special. All during the week the family has come together for the Kwanzaa ceremony. On the sixth day, many families join together. They often meet at a community center.

There is a feast called Karamu (kah-RAH-moo). It is a big celebration. People bring African food to share. There might be peanut soup, collard greens, chicken, fish, black-eyed peas, fruit, and bread.

During Kwanzaa, African Americans enjoy eating traditional African foods, such as those pictured here.

The room is decorated with black, red, and green banners. A large straw mat is placed on the floor. The candle holder, basket of fruit and vegetables, cup, ears of corn, and gifts are put on the mat. Plates of food are also placed on the mat.

The first five candles are lit. Then another red candle is lit. People talk about being creative. Everyone tells what they can do or make. They talk about how they can make their neighborhood more beautiful. A man tells about the chair he fixed. A woman talks about the clothes she is making for her children.

Through music, plays, dancing, art, storytelling, and poetry people are creative. By being creative, people make their lives more beautiful.

Then the ceremony with the cup takes place. Family members are honored and remembered.

Some people call out names of famous African Americans. Someone may give a speech. She may talk about heros like Mary McLeod Bethune, Frederick Douglass, and Martin Luther King, Jr.

After the speech, it is time to share the meal. All help themselves to food. There is always more than enough. This is a happy time with talking and laughing.

After the meal, there is African music and dancing. The dancers wear African clothes. The dances tell stories. Some dances give thanks for

This girl is wearing a mask. It has been painted on her with white paint. Her cap is decorated with shells. African dancers wear caps and masks like hers.

Music is a big part of the Kwanzaa celebration. After dinner musicians play and people sing.

the rain and crops. Some are harvest or victory dances. Music is played on many diffcrent drums.

Some families like to sing together. Other families know how to do some of the African dances. There can be music and dances any night of Kwanzaa. There is always music and dancing at the big feast on December 31.

At last it is time to give the children their gifts. These gifts can be given anytime during Kwanzaa, but most families wait until the sixth day. Children work all year to earn their gifts. They try to remember the seven principles.

Zawadi are the gifts given during Kwanzaa.

Each child receives two gifts. One is always a book. The other gift might be an African picture or carving. It might be something that belonged to a relative.

After the children open their gifts, everyone sings. They are happy to be with each other.

◆▐▪▪▪▐◆▐▪▪▪▐◆

January 1—the seventh day of Kwanzaa
Imani (ee-MAH-nee)
Imani means believing.

People need to believe in themselves and other people. They need faith in their future. Almost everyone believes in God.

Imani begins just after Kuumba ends at midnight. It is January 1 of the new year. The singing and dancing stop. Six candles are already lit. The last candle is lit. Now all seven candles are burning. People talk about what they believe. Some talk about God. They talk about the need to believe in themselves.

Children need to believe in their parents, teachers, and leaders.

They talk about the year that has just ended. What mistakes did they make? What can they do in the new year? What goals do they have? What changes will they make?

For the last time, water or juice is poured from the cup. The cup is raised. "Harambee!" Everyone shouts back "Harambee!" seven times.

Kwanzaa is over for the year, but it is not the end of thinking about the seven principles. African Americans try to live by them every day.

The seven symbols of Kwanzaa are placed in the center of the table.

Kwanzaa Symbols

There are seven things used as symbols during Kwanzaa. They are things people might have in their homes. Each one stands for an idea or for people. For Kwanzaa they are given special meanings. They are also given Swahili names.

Mkeka (mm-KAY-kah)

The Mkeka is a straw mat. It stands for African American history and ideas.

Kinara (kee-NAR-ah)

The Kinara is a candle holder. It stands for the family members who have died. It holds seven candles.

Mishumaa Saba (mi-shu-MAH SAH-ba)

There are seven candles used during Kwanzaa: one black, three red, and three green. They stand for the seven principles.

Muhindi (moo-HI-ndee)

Muhindi are ears of corn. They stand for children. One ear of corn is placed on the mat for each child in the family. If there are no children, one ear of corn is still put on the mat. This shows that children are important to everyone.

Mazao (mah-ZAH-o)

Mazao are fruits and vegetables. They stand for the harvest.

Kikombe Cha Umoja
(ki-KOHM-bay cha oo-MO-jah)

The Kikombe Cha Umoja is a cup. Kikombe means cup. The full name means unity cup.

Zawadi (zah-WAH-dee)

Zawadi are gifts. There are always two gifts given to each child. One must be a book. The other gift can be something from Africa. It could also be something that belonged to a family member.

The flag is another symbol. It stands for all African Americans. It has three broad stripes. The colors are black, red, and green. The colors stand for the African American people, their struggles, and their hopes.

The African American flag was made by Marcus Garvey. Garvey was a famous African American leader. He lived a long time ago. He made people proud of their African past.

During Kwanzaa, families display the flag. They also decorate their homes with its colors.

People decorate their homes for Kwanzaa. They display the colors of the flag: black, red, and green.

Things to Do During Kwanzaa

There are many things to see and hear during Kwanzaa. Museums show African art. Dancers perform African dances. There are plays and puppet shows about Kwanzaa.

During Kwanzaa, African Americans have a special greeting. They say, "Habari Gani" (hah-BAR-ree GAH-nee). This means "What's new?" A person answers with the principle of the day.

Sometimes friends send each other Kwanzaa cards. The cards are bright with the three Kwanzaa colors. Some people make their own Kwanzaa cards.

In one city, there is a large Kwanzaa parade. Over 20,000 people march in it. Everyone wears African masks and robes. They play African music. As the parade passes, other people join in. Finally the parade ends in a park. There is food and music for everyone.

In other cities, there are classes for children. Some of these classes teach children how to play the drums. Other classes teach them some of the dances.

This girl is at a workshop at a cultural center. She is making a Zawadi to give her father on the last day of Kwanzaa.

During December some children learn about Kwanzaa in their schools. They play African games. They make African crafts. They learn about African countries.

They talk about making the world a better place by using the seven principles.

The first Kwanzaa was celebrated by Dr. Karenga and a few friends. Now millions of African Americans celebrate this holiday. Every year more people learn about Kwanzaa. Dr. Karenga's idea has spread. African Americans look forward to the last week of December. It is a time for learning. It is a time to be proud. It is a time for sharing. It is also a time for fun and joy. In one of his books, Dr. Karenga says, "May the year's end meet us laughing and stronger . . ."

HARAMBEE!   HARAMBEE!
HARAMBEE!
HARAMBEE!   HARAMBEE!
HARAMBEE!   HARAMBEE!

Kwanzaa is a time for learning, sharing, fun, and joy!

Nguzo Saba—The Seven Principles

1. **Umoja** (oo-MO-jah)—Being united or joined together.

2. **Kujichagulia** (koo-jee-cha-goo-LEE-ah)— Being yourself. Thinking for yourself; deciding what you are going to do and say.

3. **Ujima** (oo-JEE-mah)—Working together to help people.

4. **Ujamaa** (oo-jah-MAH)—Sharing work and wealth.

5. **Nia** (NEE-ah)—Having a purpose or reason for doing something; having a goal.

6. **Kuumba** (koo-UH-mbah)—Being creative; making something new.

7. **Imani** (ee-MAH-nee)—Having faith. Believing in people and God.

Glossary

---

ceremony—A celebration always done in the same way.

creative—To make something new.

Habari Gani—Swahili words that mean "What's new?"

Harambee—The Swahili word that means "Let's all pull together."

Karamu—A Swahili word for the large feast on the sixth day of Kwanzaa.

kwanza—The Swahili word that stands for the first fruits picked at harvest time in Africa.

Kwanzaa—The African American holiday celebrated each year from December 26 through January 1.

museum—A building where things of art, science, or history are kept.

Nguzo Saba—The Swahili words for "seven principles." They are used to mean the seven rules of Kwanzaa.

plantain—A fruit similar to a banana.

principle—A rule of behavior that a person chooses to live by.

purpose—The reason for which something is made or done.

struggle—To make a great effort, to fight strong opposition.

Swahili—An African language spoken in thirteen African countries and understood by many Africans.

symbol—A thing that stands for an idea.

Note to Parents, Teachers, and Librarians

In this book, words within the vocabularies of younger children are used to define the Swahili words. The following list gives the literal meaning of the Swahili terms, as translated by Dr. Maulana Karenga.

1. **Umoja**—Unity

2. **Kujichagulia**—Self-determination

3. **Ujima**—Collective Work and Responsibility

4. **Ujamaa**—Cooperative Economics

5. **Nia**—Purpose

6. **Kuumba**—Creativity

7. **Imani**—Faith

Index